Frontiers of Europe

Russia of the Czars

Portugal of the Navigators

Imperial Visions
The Rise and Fall of Empires

Frontiers of Europe

Russia of the Czars

Portugal of the Navigators

Joyce Milton
Russia of the Czars

Henry Wiencek
Portugal of the Navigators

Preface by James Miller
Assistant Professor of History
Stockton State College

HBJ Press
a subsidiary of Harcourt Brace Jovanovich
New York, New York

HBJ Press

Publisher, John R. Whitman
Executive Editor, Marcia Heath
Managing Editor, Janice Lemmo
Series Editors: John Radziewicz, Suzanne Stewart
Editorial Production, Hope Keller

Marketing Staff: Mark A. Mayer, Jose J. Elizalde, Laurie Farber

Authors: Joyce Milton, Henry Wiencek
Picture Researcher, Janet Adams

Consultants
    Russia of the Czars: Professor James Miller
    Portugal of the Navigators: Professor Kenneth Maxwell

Design Implementation, Designworks

Rizzoli Editore

Authors of the Italian Edition
    Introduction: Professor Ovidio Dallera
    Russia of the Czars: Professor Pacifico Montanari
    Portugal of the Navigators: Professor Angela Sala
    Maps: Gian Franco Leonardi
Idea and Realization, Harry C. Lindinger
Graphic Design, Gerry Valsecchi
General Editorial Supervisor, Ovidio Dallera

© 1980 by Rizzoli Editore
Printed in Italy.

Library of Congress Cataloging in Publication Data
Main entry under title:

Frontiers of Europe.

    (Imperial visions)
    Includes index.
    CONTENTS: Milton, J. Russia of the czars.—
Wiencek, H. Portugal of the navigators.
    1. Russia—Civilization. 2. Portugal—Civilization.
I. Milton, Joyce. Russia of the czars. 1980.
II. Wiencek, Henry. Portugal of the navigators. 1980.
III. Series.
DK32.F76   946.9   79-2527
ISBN 0-15-004033-4